A Parent's Guide to an Autism Friendly Christmas

Practical Tips for Calm, Connection and Celebration This Festive Season

Sydney Clarke

STILLPATH
BOOKS

Stillpath Books

Copyright © [2025] by [Sydney Clarke]

All rights reserved.

No portion of this book may be reproduced in any form without written permission from the publisher or author, except as permitted by U.S. copyright law.

This book provides general information and strategies for supporting autistic children during Christmas. It is not intended as a substitute for professional medical, therapeutic, or educational advice. Parents should consult with qualified professionals regarding their child's specific needs.

The family stories and examples in this book are based on real experiences shared by autism families. All names and identifying details have been changed to protect privacy.

E-book ISBN: 978-1-7642438-0-3

Paperback ISBN: 978-1-7642438-1-0

Published by Stillpath Books First Edition

STILLPATH
BOOKS

Contents

1. A Different Kind of Christmas Magic — 1
2. Understanding the Christmas Challenge — 7
3. The Tinsel Tangle: Meltdowns vs Tantrums — 12
4. Deck the Halls Slowly: Mastering Christmas Transitions — 19
5. Silent Night, Peaceful Night: Creating Sensory-Smart Spaces — 25
6. The Present Puzzle: Making Gift Time Gentle — 31
7. Navigating Holiday Food — 37
8. All Together Now Maybe: Managing Family Gatherings — 43
9. Surviving the Holiday Hustle: Shopping with Sensory Smarts — 50
10. Room for All the Reindeer: Including Siblings in the Season — 57
11. Tech the Halls: Using Technology to Support Success — 67
12. Creating Your Own Kind of Merry: Autism-Friendly Holiday Traditions — 74

13. Your Family's Perfect Christmas — 82

A Different Kind of Christmas Magic

If you've picked up this book, chances are you're facing a familiar December dilemma. You want to create magical Christmas memories for your family, but you're also wondering how to navigate the season with your autistic child. Perhaps you've experienced holiday meltdowns, struggled with sensory overload at family gatherings, or felt the weight of trying to make "traditional" Christmas work when it clearly doesn't fit your family's needs.

You're not alone. And more importantly, you're not failing.

Who This Book Is For

This guide is written for parents and caregivers of autistic children and teens who want to create meaningful, joyful holiday experiences that work for their whole family. Whether your child is 4 or 14, whether they speak or communicate in other ways, whether they love Christmas lights or find them overwhelming, this book is for you.

You might be:

- A parent experiencing your first Christmas after an autism diagnosis

- A family who's struggled through difficult holiday seasons and wants a better way

- Grandparents, relatives, or friends trying to understand how to support an autism family

- An educator or professional working with autistic children during the holiday season

Its important to note that not all autistic children and families experience difficulties during the festive season. This book is for those who do!

About the Stories in This Book

Throughout this guide, you'll read stories from families navigating Christmas with their autistic children. All names and identifying details have been changed to protect privacy while sharing real experiences and solutions that have worked for families like yours. These stories combine common experiences reported by autism families with strategies that have proven successful in creating more joyful holiday celebrations.

How to Use This Book

Each chapter focuses on a specific aspect of the Christmas season, from managing sensory challenges to navigating family gatherings. You don't need to read them in order. Jump to whatever feels most relevant to your current situation.

Each chapter includes real family examples, practical strategies, and guidance on recognizing when approaches need adjusting.

You'll find strategy summaries at the end of each chapter for quick reference.

The Heart of This Journey

Before we dive into specific strategies, I want you to know something important: your family's Christmas doesn't need to look like anyone else's to be beautiful. Some of the most magical Christmases involve families who open presents on December 15th because waiting is too stressful, families who celebrate with pizza instead of turkey because that's what their child can eat, and families who skip the big gatherings and create quiet, sensory-friendly moments at home.

There's no "right" way to celebrate Christmas. There's only your family's way. And when your family's way honors each person's needs and celebrates everyone's unique qualities, that's not just a successful holiday. That's a beautiful way to live.

About the Research

The strategies shared in this book are grounded in current research on autism, sensory processing, family dynamics, and child development. While I haven't included formal citations to maintain readability and keep the focus on practical guidance, these approaches align with evidence-based practices widely recognized in autism support.

The understanding of autistic experiences has evolved significantly over the past decades, moving from deficit-focused models to strength-based, neurodiversity-affirming approaches. This book reflects current best practices that prioritize:

Accommodation over adaptation: Research consistently shows that modifying environments to meet autistic needs is more effective than expecting autistic individuals to adapt to overwhelming situations.

Preparation and predictability: Studies demonstrate that advance planning, visual supports, and clear expectations significantly reduce anxiety and improve participation.

Sensory-informed approaches: Growing evidence highlights the central role of sensory processing differences in autistic experiences, particularly during high-stimulation periods like holidays.

Family-centered strategies: Research emphasizes the importance of supporting entire families, including siblings, rather than focusing solely on the autistic individual.

Authentic participation: Evidence supports celebrating genuine responses and interests rather than teaching compliance or "appropriate" behaviors.

The family stories throughout this book represent common experiences reported by autism families, combined with strategies that have been tested and refined through both research and real-world application. Every suggestion has been shaped by listening to autistic voices, supporting families through challenging times, and staying current with evolving best practices in autism support.

Most importantly, this book recognizes that each autistic person is unique. While research provides valuable guidance, your intimate knowledge of your child remains the most important factor in creating successful holiday experiences.

Your Child's Unique Gifts

Your autistic child brings special qualities to the Christmas season that often go unrecognized or undervalued. Their attention to detail might help them notice beauty in decorations that others miss. Their honest emotions mean that when joy comes, it's genuine and unfiltered. Their strong memory for meaningful moments can help establish family traditions once you find what works. Their unique perspectives can enrich your family's experience in unexpected ways.

The goal isn't to make your child more "Christmas-ready." It's to make Christmas more accessible to your child so they can share their authentic self with your family during this special time.

Moving Forward Together

As we explore specific strategies in the following chapters, remember that you're not trying to fix anything that's broken. You're learning to create space where your child can experience genuine enjoyment rather than just survival. You're discovering how to build celebrations around your family's actual needs rather than external expectations.

Some strategies will work perfectly for your family. Others might need tweaking. A few might not fit at all, and that's completely fine. Take what serves you, adapt what might work with changes, and leave what doesn't fit.

Your journey through this book is really a journey toward understanding that different doesn't mean less magical. In fact, when families embrace their unique needs and strengths, they often discover that their celebrations become more meaningful, more joyful, and more authentically connected than they ever imagined possible.

A Note on Language: This book uses identity-first language ("autistic person" rather than "person with autism") as preferred by many autistic self-advocates and the broader autistic community. We recognize that some families prefer person-first language, and both approaches come from a place of respect and love. What matters most is supporting your family in the way that works best for you.

Understanding the Christmas Challenge

If you've picked up this book, you're likely feeling that familiar December tension between wanting to create magic while worrying about meltdowns, hoping for joy while preparing for challenges. This chapter will help you understand why Christmas feels so complex for autistic children, so you can approach the season with confidence rather than anxiety.

The Hidden Complexity of Christmas

Last December, Sarah watched her 8-year-old son Marcus at their family Christmas party. To everyone else, he seemed fine. He smiled for photos, said thank you for gifts, even hugged his grandmother. But Sarah knew better. She could see the tight grip on his comfort toy, the way he flinched at unexpected laughter, how he kept checking the time on her phone.

Two hours later, safe in their car, Marcus completely fell apart.

"I don't understand," Sarah's mother-in-law said later. "He seemed so happy at the party."

This is the reality parents face: their autistic child appears to be coping beautifully while actually working incredibly hard just to survive the experience.

Why Christmas Hits Differently

Christmas doesn't just add excitement to an autistic child's world. It fundamentally changes everything they rely on for security and comfort.

The Sensory Explosion Your child's nervous system processes sensory information differently. During Christmas, this difference becomes overwhelming. A typical room during the holidays transforms: bright lights flash in patterns, music plays constantly, new smells from cooking and candles fill the air, different textures appear on clothes and decorations, and people move and speak more excitedly than usual.

For your child, this isn't just "festive." It's like trying to concentrate while someone randomly adjusts the volume, brightness, and temperature of their environment every few minutes.

When Routine Becomes Optional School schedules disappear overnight. Bedtimes shift for family events. Meal times change around gatherings. The predictable rhythm that helps your child feel secure simply vanishes, replaced by "we'll see how it goes" and "it depends."

Social Expectations Multiply Suddenly there are new rules about hugging relatives, showing excitement for gifts you might not want, sitting still through longer meals, and being "on" for extended periods. The social energy required increases dramatically just when the supports that usually help are disrupted.

The Exhausting Work of Masking

Many autistic children engage in masking, whereby they consciously suppress their autistic traits in order to fit in with those around them. This may include copying social behaviors, forcing eye contact or conversational styles that are uncomfortable for them. Understanding m*asking* reveals that masking requires enormous energy.

Marcus's story illustrates this perfectly. His mother Jennifer learned to read the signs: "Marcus would hold it together beautifully at Christmas parties. He'd say thank you for gifts, hug relatives, participate in activities. But I could see the cost. His hands would shake slightly when he thought no one was looking. He'd excuse himself to the bathroom repeatedly, just for quiet moments. By the time we got to the car, he was completely depleted. It took me three Christmases to realize that what looked like social success was actually exhaustion."

This invisible effort is called masking, and it requires enormous mental energy. During Christmas, when the pressure to appear grateful, social, and happy intensifies, this exhaustion compounds daily.

When Other Conditions Complicate Christmas

About 70% of autistic children have at least one additional condition that affects how they experience the holidays.

ADHD Plus Autism The excitement of Christmas can trigger ADHD hyperactivity just when your child's autistic nervous system needs calm. Impulse control becomes harder around presents and activities, while the need for predictability increases. It's like having one foot on the gas and one on the brake.

Anxiety Plus Autism Christmas anticipation becomes Christmas dread. Worry about unknown social situations, fear of sensory overload, and anxiety about disappointing others can start weeks before any actual events. The "what ifs" multiply exponentially.

What Actually Helps

Research consistently shows that autistic children thrive when their environment becomes more predictable, not when they're expected to become more flexible.

Preparation Over Surprises Visual schedules, social stories, and advance planning reduce anxiety more effectively than trying to build "tolerance" for unpredictability.

Accommodation Over Adaptation Modifying the environment to meet your child's sensory needs works better than hoping they'll "get used to" overwhelming situations.

Authentic Joy Over Performed Happiness Creating space for your child's genuine responses, even if they don't match traditional expectations, leads to more meaningful celebrations than forcing artificial enthusiasm.

Building on Your Child's Strengths

Your autistic child brings unique gifts to Christmas that often go unrecognized. Ten-year-old Emma's attention to detail amazes her family. "She notices things about our decorations that we completely miss," her mom shares. "The way the light hits the ornaments, patterns in the wrapping paper, how the tree lights reflect in the window. Her joy, when it comes, is so genuine it makes everyone else happier too."

Moving Forward

The goal isn't to eliminate all challenges from Christmas. It's to understand what your child is experiencing so you can create celebrations that honor who they truly are.

Key Takeaways:

- Christmas challenges every system your autistic child relies on for security

- "Looking fine" often means working incredibly hard to cope

- Additional conditions like ADHD and anxiety compound holiday stress

- Accommodation works better than expecting adaptation

- Your child's authentic responses are more valuable than performed happiness

The Tinsel Tangle: Meltdowns vs Tantrums

Building from Chapter 1: Now that you understand why Christmas is challenging for autistic children, you're ready to tackle one of parents' biggest concerns: distinguishing between meltdowns and tantrums. This knowledge can transform how your family navigates difficult moments during the holiday season.

The Critical Difference

Last Christmas morning, 7-year-old Tom seemed excited about presents. He'd helped arrange them under the tree the night before and woke up eager to begin. But after opening three gifts with everyone watching and commenting, plus the dog barking and Christmas music playing, he suddenly started screaming and couldn't stop.

His father tried offering Tom's favorite toy, his preferred snack, even promising he could open more presents. Nothing worked.

"He wasn't trying to get anything," Tom's dad explains. "His nervous system was just completely overwhelmed."

This is the difference between a meltdown and a tantrum, and understanding it changes everything about how you respond.

Understanding Tantrums

Think of a tantrum like a negotiation tactic. When a child has a tantrum, they're usually trying to achieve something specific: get a desired item, avoid an unwanted task, gain attention, or test boundaries.

Tantrums have these characteristics:

- Have a clear goal or desired outcome
- Can often be reasoned with or distracted
- Usually stop when the goal is achieved or clearly won't be met
- The child maintains some control and awareness
- Can be "turned off" if something better comes along

Understanding Meltdowns

A meltdown is fundamentally different. It's not a choice or strategy, but a neurological response to overwhelm. Think of it like a circuit breaker that trips when the electrical system is overloaded. The meltdown is the brain's way of protecting itself from damage.

Meltdowns have these characteristics:

- Happen when the nervous system reaches overload
- Cannot be reasoned with or negotiated during the episode
- Don't stop when offered rewards or consequences

- The child has little to no control during the episode

- Often followed by exhaustion or shame

- Can be triggered by seemingly small events if pressure has been building

Christmas: The Perfect Storm

Christmas creates an ideal environment for meltdowns because it combines virtually every challenge that can overwhelm an autistic nervous system.

Sensory Bombardment Jennifer's 9-year-old daughter Emma experienced this at their family gathering. "Within an hour of arriving, Emma was overwhelmed. I realized what she'd processed: new people talking loudly, cinnamon candles burning, Christmas music, her scratchy new sweater, and the smell of turkey. All while being expected to be social and grateful. Her sensory cup just overflowed."

Routine Destruction Christmas systematically dismantles the routines that help autistic children feel secure. Schools close, sleep schedules shift, meal times change, and familiar activities disappear.

Social and Emotional Pressure The social expectations of Christmas can be overwhelming: expected enthusiasm and gratitude, physical affection with extended family, social reciprocity in gift giving, "appropriate" emotional responses, extended social interactions, and performance of happiness.

Recognizing the Warning Signs

Meltdowns rarely happen without warning. Learning to recognize

Silent Night, Peaceful Night: Creating Sensory-Smart Spaces

Building on transition mastery: You've learned how to introduce Christmas changes gradually. Now we'll focus on creating physical environments that support your child's sensory needs while maintaining holiday magic.

Understanding Christmas Sensory Overload

Imagine walking into a typical Christmas gathering and experiencing every sensation amplified. Every splash of laughter becomes thunderous, every twinkling light feels like a strobe, every perfume or food smell overwhelms, and every fabric texture feels exaggerated. This is how Christmas can feel for your autistic child.

Christmas creates what specialists call a "sensory cocktail," a mix of intense experiences that can quickly become overwhelming. Twinkling lights flash in complex patterns, carols compete with conversation, unfamiliar foods create new smells, different textures appear in decorations and clothes, and there's an expectation to navigate this sensory bombardment while being social and grateful.

your child's specific early indicators can help you intervene before they reach the point of no return.

Emma's mother Sarah learned to watch for specific signs: "Emma gets very quiet and starts organizing things obsessively when she's getting overwhelmed. If I see her lining up Christmas ornaments or asking the same question about Santa's schedule repeatedly, I know it's time for a sensory break."

Early warning signs include:

- Increased stimming behaviors
- Seeking quiet or isolated spaces
- Covering ears or eyes
- Becoming more rigid about small rules
- Decreased tolerance for normal sounds or touch
- Difficulty with transitions
- Asking repetitive questions
- Changes in speech patterns or volume

Prevention Strategies That Work

Managing Sensory Load The Wilson family developed what they call "Sensory Banking." Max's dad explains: "We think of Max's sensory system like a bank account. We make 'deposits' by providing calming sensory input and manage 'withdrawals' by controlling overwhelming input. Before Christmas events, we make sure his sensory account has a positive balance."

Practical sensory management includes:

- Pre-loading calm input with weighted blanket time, favorite music, familiar scents
- Environmental control by dimming lights, reducing background noise, maintaining comfortable temperature
- Having sensory tools ready like noise-canceling headphones, fidget toys, comfort items
- Planning regular breaks to retreat to quiet spaces
- Gradual exposure by slowly increasing holiday stimulation rather than sudden immersion

Routine Anchoring Rather than abandoning all routines, create "anchor points" of familiarity within the holiday chaos. The Martinez family kept Miguel's morning routine exactly the same throughout the holidays. "Everything else could change, but he still woke up, had the same breakfast, and did his morning puzzle. Those 45 minutes of familiarity helped him handle the rest of the day's changes."

Communication and Preparation Alex's family created "Christmas Intel Briefings." Before any holiday event, they walk through exactly what will happen, who will be there, what sounds and smells to expect, and what their escape plan is. Alex helps create the plan, so he feels in control rather than surprised.

During a Meltdown: What to Do

Stay Calm Your energy directly affects your child's ability to recover. Emma's mom learned this the hard way: "My first instinct was to solve the problem by offering her favorite food, or turning on her favorite show. But that just added more pressure. When I learned to just sit quietly nearby and wait, her meltdowns became shorter and less intense."

Ensure Safety Remove harmful objects and create space. Provide comfort through weighted blankets, gentle pressure, or familiar music.

Wait It Out Meltdowns have to run their course. Use minimal words like "You're safe," "I'm here," or "This will pass."

What Not to Do Don't try to reason or teach during the meltdown, add more sensory input through talking or touching, make demands or give instructions, take it personally or feel embarrassed, or punish the meltdown.

The Recovery Phase

After a meltdown, autistic children often experience physical and emotional exhaustion, possible shame or embarrassment, need for comfort and reassurance, gradual return to baseline functioning, and possible lingering sensory sensitivity.

Support recovery by providing a quiet, low-stimulation environment, offering comfort items and preferred activities, avoiding discussion of the meltdown immediately, maintaining normal routines as much as possible, and planning for a lighter schedule for the rest of the day.

Moving Toward Success

Understanding the difference between meltdowns and tantrums isn't just academic knowledge. It's the foundation for creating a Christmas where your child can participate authentically rather than just survive.

Quick Reference Guide:

Tantrum (Goal Oriented):

- Stops when goal is met or denied
- Can be reasoned with or distracted
- Child maintains some control
- Has clear desired outcome

Meltdown (Nervous System Overload):

- Must run its course regardless of offers
- Cannot be reasoned with during episode
- Child has little to no control
- Is a response to overwhelm, not wanting something
- Requires recovery time after it ends

Deck the Halls Slowly: Mastering Christmas Transitions

Building on your new understanding of meltdowns: One of the biggest meltdown triggers during Christmas is transitions. This chapter will show you how to build bridges between your child's need for routine and the necessary changes that come with the holiday season.

Why Transitions Feel Like Earthquakes

For autistic children, routines aren't just habits. They're vital navigation tools, like having a GPS for daily life. The predictability of knowing breakfast follows waking up, or that homework happens after school, creates a sense of security and control.

When Christmas arrives, it's like someone has suddenly recalibrated their GPS with new routes, destinations, and expectations. Nine-year-old Jake's mom describes it perfectly: "Imagine if your work schedule was completely erased tomorrow and replaced with a series of unpredictable events. That's what the holiday break feels like for Jake."

The Holiday Transition Challenge

Christmas presents several major transition challenges that can accumulate into overwhelm:

School-to-Holiday Shift The familiar rhythm of classes, break times, and regular interactions suddenly disappears, replaced by unstructured time and unpredictable activities.

Home Environment Changes Spaces that usually provide comfort and predictability start changing. Christmas trees appear in familiar corners, furniture gets rearranged, and new decorations bring different textures, lights, and sounds.

Activity Pattern Disruption Mealtimes become irregular, bedtime routines flex around events, and there are new social expectations to navigate.

Building Bridges to Christmas

Rather than diving straight into holiday chaos, think of the transition like building a bridge between your regular routine and your holiday schedule. The key is starting construction early, about 2-3 weeks before major changes begin.

Creating a Christmas Command Center This becomes a visual guide to upcoming changes. For younger children, this might be a simple calendar with pictures showing when decorations will appear or when special events will happen. Older children might prefer a more detailed schedule. The crucial element is involving your child in the planning process, letting them help decide which parts of their regular routine they'd like to keep during the holidays.

Real Success Stories

The Wilson Family's Step-Down Approach Tom's parents discovered that gradual change prevented overwhelm. "Instead of switching everything to holiday mode at once, we introduced changes slowly. Week one, we kept our morning routine exactly the same but added one holiday activity each afternoon. Week two, we modified dinner time slightly while maintaining breakfast and bedtime routines. By Christmas week, Tom felt secure enough to handle bigger changes because he still had familiar anchors."

The Martinez Family's Zone Method Carlos's family created different areas in their house with varying levels of Christmas intensity. "We kept Carlos's bedroom completely decoration-free as his 'calm zone.' The kitchen remained mostly normal. But we went full festive in the family room, where Carlos could choose to engage with more intense holiday experiences when he felt ready. Having spaces that stayed familiar gave him control over his sensory exposure."

Practical Transition Strategies

Advance Preparation Start planning and discussing changes 2-3 weeks early. Take photos of planned decorations or activities so your child can process what's coming. Create visual schedules showing both what will change and what will stay the same.

Routine Anchoring Keep some routines completely unchanged throughout the holiday period. This might be the morning sequence, bedtime routine, or specific meal patterns. These become your child's "home base" during the chaos.

Gradual Introduction Instead of transforming your house overnight, introduce holiday elements slowly. Add decorations to one room per week. Start playing holiday music for short periods. Gradually increase the "Christmas level" of your environment.

Practice Sessions Rehearse transitions during calm times. If you're visiting relatives, drive by their house before the event. Practice greeting scenarios. Role-play gift opening. Familiarity reduces anxiety.

When Overwhelm Strikes

Even with careful planning, there will be moments when holiday changes become too much. That's when your "rescue routine" comes into play. This is a short sequence of familiar activities your child can return to when feeling overwhelmed.

For Emma, it's spending ten minutes with her favorite weighted blanket and a familiar book in her calm zone. For Marcus, it's organizing his collection of small cars while listening to his preferred playlist. The key is having these routines practiced and ready before you need them.

Recognizing When Adjustments Are Needed

Watch for signs that your approach needs modification: increased anxiety about upcoming events, sleep disruption that wasn't present before, meltdowns increasing in frequency or intensity, withdrawal from activities they usually enjoy, or increased rigidity about unchanged routines.

These signals tell you that the pace of change might be too fast, or that more routine anchors are needed, or that additional sensory support is required during transitions.

Creating Your Family's Transition Plan

Week 1: Foundation Maintain all current routines while introducing the idea of upcoming changes. Show photos, read books about Christmas, discuss what will happen.

Week 2: Gentle Changes Begin decorating one area while keeping others normal. Start playing holiday music for short periods. Introduce one new holiday activity while maintaining regular activities.

Week 3: Building Momentum Add more decorations and activities while monitoring your child's comfort level. Practice any special routines for upcoming events. Increase holiday elements gradually.

Christmas Week: Full Experience Your child is now prepared for the full Christmas experience because the changes have been introduced gradually and familiar elements remain constant.

Tools for Success

Visual Schedules: Create picture schedules showing the sequence of holiday activities and when regular routines will return.

Transition Warnings: Give specific time warnings before changes. "In 15 minutes, we'll start decorating the tree. First we'll move the coffee table, then we'll put on the lights."

Choice and Control: Offer choices whenever possible. "Would you like to help hang ornaments or would you prefer to direct where they go?"

Escape Routes: Always have a plan for your child to remove themselves from overwhelming situations without stigma or consequence.

Moving Forward

Successful holiday transitions aren't about eliminating all changes. They're about introducing changes in a way that feels manageable and predictable. When your child knows what's coming and has familiar routines to anchor them, they can enjoy the magic of Christmas rather than just survive it.

Transition Success Checklist:

- Start planning 2 to 3 weeks early
- Keep some routines completely unchanged
- Introduce changes gradually
- Practice new activities during calm times
- Have rescue routines ready for overwhelm
- Give your child choices and control when possible
- Watch for signs that adjustments are needed

Creating Your Sensory-Safe Haven

The key to managing Christmas sensory challenges isn't about eliminating all holiday cheer. It's about creating environments where your child can enjoy the season without becoming overwhelmed.

The Zone Approach Jenny transformed their house into what she calls "sensory zones" for her 9-year-old son Alex. "We created different areas with varying levels of Christmas intensity. The living room has gentle, steady lights and minimal decorations. The kitchen is completely decoration-free. It's our 'neutral zone.' But we went full festive in the family room, where Alex can choose to engage with more intense holiday experiences when he feels ready."

This approach gives children control over their sensory exposure. They can enjoy Christmas decorations when they want stimulation and retreat to calm spaces when they need relief.

Room-by-Room Sensory Solutions

The Calm Room Every home needs what families call a "low-arousal space." For Marcus's family, this meant keeping his bedroom completely free of holiday changes. "It's his sanctuary," his mother explains. "When everything else feels too much, he knows his room stays exactly the same. We put his Christmas gifts there after he opens them, so it becomes associated with joy rather than overwhelm."

Living Spaces Consider these gentler approaches to traditional decorations:

- Replace blinking lights with steady, warm white LEDs

- Choose decorations in calming colors rather than bright, contrasting ones

- Use battery-operated candles for gentle lighting without flicker

- Create clear pathways through rooms to avoid crowding

- Maintain familiar furniture arrangements where possible

Sensory Relief Stations Sarah created what she calls "sensory pit stops" around their house for her daughter Emma. "We have little corners with comfort items. Her favorite weighted blanket, noise-canceling headphones, and fidget toys. They're like refueling stations when she starts feeling overwhelmed. The key is having them readily available without Emma having to ask for help or explain what she needs."

Managing Multi-Sensory Challenges

Light Management Christmas lighting often triggers sensory difficulties. Rather than traditional flashing displays, try:

- Using warm white LEDs instead of multicolored ones

- Creating lighting zones with different intensities throughout your home

- Installing dimmer switches for better control throughout the day

- Maximizing natural light during daytime hours

- Setting timers to maintain predictable lighting patterns

Sound Solutions The cacophony of Christmas can be particularly challenging. Create sound-smart spaces by:

- Designating specific quiet zones in your home

- Using soft furnishings like cushions and blankets to absorb noise

- Playing familiar background music at low volumes rather than holiday music exclusively

- Having noise-canceling headphones readily available without stigma

- Creating sound barriers between active and quiet areas

Smell Considerations Holiday scents can trigger sensory overload. Consider:

- Keeping strongly scented items like candles or potpourri in contained areas

- Using natural scents like pine or vanilla rather than artificial fragrances

- Maintaining good ventilation throughout your home

- Creating scent-free zones for relief

- Introducing new smells gradually rather than all at once

Helping Guests Understand

When visitors arrive, help them understand and respect your sensory-smart space. Marie sends a gentle note to guests before gatherings for her 11-year-old daughter Emma: "We explain our 'quiet house' approach and how it helps Emma enjoy family gatherings more. We mention that she might wear headphones sometimes, that there are specific calm spaces she might retreat to, and that this helps her participate more fully rather than less. Most people are wonderfully understanding when they know why."

Recognizing Sensory Overload

Watch for these indicators that your space needs sensory adjustment:

- Covering ears or eyes more frequently
- Seeking dark or quiet spaces repeatedly
- Becoming more active or withdrawn than usual
- Changes in breathing patterns or increased fidgeting
- Difficulty with normal transitions
- Increased need for familiar comfort items

Portable Sensory Solutions

Not every Christmas activity happens in your carefully designed home environment. Create portable sensory support systems:

- Small backpacks with essential sensory tools
- Noise-canceling headphones that connect to tablets or phones
- Weighted lap pads that can be used anywhere
- Familiar scents in small containers
- Fidget tools that work in various environments

Building Sensory Success

Creating sensory-smart Christmas spaces isn't about diminishing holiday spirit. It's about making celebrations accessible and enjoyable for everyone in your family. When your child can regulate their sensory input, they're more likely to engage with family activities, enjoy holiday traditions, and create positive Christmas memories.

The goal is balance: enough holiday magic to feel festive, enough sensory control to feel safe, and enough flexibility to adjust as needed.

Sensory Environment Checklist:

- Create zones with different sensory intensities
- Provide readily accessible calm spaces
- Use steady lighting rather than flashing
- Maintain quiet zones alongside active areas
- Keep familiar scents and minimize artificial ones
- Have portable sensory tools ready for outings
- Educate guests about your family's sensory needs

The Present Puzzle: Making Gift Time Gentle

Building on sensory awareness: Now that you understand how to create supportive environments, let's tackle one of Christmas's most complex challenges: gift giving and receiving. This combines sensory, social, and emotional demands in ways that can overwhelm even well prepared children.

Understanding the Gift Challenge

Gift time combines almost every Christmas difficulty into one intense experience. The sensory overload from wrapping paper sounds and visual stimulation, the social pressure to react "appropriately," the unpredictability of surprises, and the performance expectations from watching family members all converge during present opening.

Emma's mom explains the complexity: "Everyone expects that magical Christmas morning reaction. But for Emma, surprises are stressful, not exciting. She needs time to process each gift, and her genuine reactions don't always match what people expect to see. We had to learn that authentic appreciation looks different from performed enthusiasm."

The Challenge of Surprises

For children who thrive on predictability, surprises can feel threatening rather than exciting. The anticipation creates anxiety, the unknown outcome feels unsafe, and the pressure to react immediately feels overwhelming.

The Anderson Family's Preview Solution James's dad revolutionized their gift-giving with "Preview and Prepare." They take photos of James's gifts before wrapping them. "He can look through the pictures beforehand, process what's coming, and genuine excitement builds naturally. On Christmas morning, he knows what to expect but still enjoys the actual moment of receiving. The element of surprise wasn't bringing joy, so we replaced it with the joy of anticipation."

Practice Makes Comfortable

David's family discovered the power of rehearsal. "We practice gift opening in November. We wrap up some of his regular toys and practice the whole routine. How to say thank you, what to do with wrapping paper, how to ask for help opening difficult packages. By Christmas, the process feels familiar instead of scary."

This approach removes the performance pressure and allows children to focus on enjoying the gifts rather than managing the social complexities of receiving them.

Setting Up For Success

Sensory-Smart Wrapping Consider your child's sensory preferences:

- Use gift bags instead of crinkly wrapping paper for texture-sensitive children

- Choose wrapping paper without loud colors, busy patterns, or metallic materials

- Minimize tape usage for easier opening

- Consider fabric wraps that feel softer and can be reused

The Gift Station Approach Sarah created a "Gift Station" for her son Tom. "We have a quiet corner where Tom can open presents at his own pace. He has his comfort items nearby, and we space out the gift-opening throughout the day rather than all at once. There's no audience pressure, no time constraints, and he can process each gift fully before moving to the next."

Managing the Gift Opening Process

One at a Time Method Max's mom learned that multiple presents create overwhelm. "We used to put all his gifts under the tree at once. Max would take one look at the pile and shut down. Now we bring out one gift at a time. He can fully experience and enjoy each one before moving to the next. It's made Christmas morning so much more joyful for everyone."

The Station Method Tom's family sets up different "gift stations" around their house. Each station has one gift and space to explore it. Tom moves between stations at his own pace, spending as much time as he wants with each present. "It spreads out the sensory experience and gives him control over the timing," his mom explains.

When Gifts Don't Land as Expected

Even with careful preparation, sometimes gifts don't match expectations or preferences.

The Neutral Response Strategy Lauren practiced simple, acceptable responses with her son: "We developed phrases like 'Thank you for thinking of me' or 'This is interesting.' It gives him something appropriate to say while he processes his real feelings privately. No one expects elaborate enthusiasm, and he doesn't feel pressure to perform emotions he's not feeling."

The Processing Time Approach Emma's mom allows time for delayed appreciation. "Emma knows she can say 'I need to think about this' and set a gift aside. Later, when she's had time to process, she often discovers she actually likes it. We've learned that immediate reactions aren't the only authentic reactions."

Teaching Meaningful Gift-Giving

Interest-Based Giving The Wilson family involves Max in choosing and creating gifts for others. "Max makes playlists for his music-loving aunt, picks out specific building sets for his cousin based on their interests. It helps him understand the meaning behind gift exchange and makes him proud to give presents he's chosen thoughtfully."

Sophie's mom discovered her daughter's love of organizing could become gift-giving strength. "Sophie creates beautiful labeled storage systems for people. It lets her use her natural talents while giving meaningful gifts that actually help family members."

Managing Family Expectations

Educating Gift-Givers Help family members understand what types of gifts work best. Maria sends relatives a simple guide:

"Items related to his interests, things with clear purposes, gifts that don't require immediate enthusiasm. Most family members appreciate the guidance rather than guessing what might work."

Setting Realistic Expectations Focus on participation over performance. The goal isn't elaborate thank-you speeches or excited jumping. The goal is your child feeling comfortable enough to engage with the gift-giving process in their own authentic way.

Emergency Strategies

When Gift Time Goes Wrong Jake's mom has learned to pause everything when overwhelm strikes. "Gifts wait. People stop talking. He gets his sensory break. Presents aren't going anywhere, but his emotional regulation is more important than maintaining the schedule."

The Escape Plan Emma knows she can say "gift break" anytime, and her family immediately stops and goes to her calm room. "Usually after 10-15 minutes, she's ready to try again. Sometimes she's done for the day, and that's okay too."

Alternative Gift Experiences

The Gift Hunt Method Sarah's family hides presents around the house with clues. "It spreads out the sensory experience and adds movement, which helps manage the intensity. Plus, Ben loves puzzles and problem-solving, so it incorporates his strengths."

The Gift Week Approach Maya's parents give one gift per day during Christmas week. "She gets to fully enjoy each present without overwhelm, and Christmas becomes a gentle celebration rather than an intense event. By December 25th, she's excited rather than anxious."

Creating Authentic Joy

The goal isn't to eliminate all challenges from gift time. It's to create opportunities for genuine enjoyment and connection around giving and receiving. When we remove the performance pressure and sensory overwhelm, children can experience the true joy of thoughtful gift exchange.

Gift Success Strategies:

- Prepare children for what to expect

- Practice gift opening during calm times

- Create sensory friendly opening environments

- Allow processing time for delayed appreciation

- Focus on authentic responses over performed enthusiasm

- Have clear escape plans for overwhelm

Navigating Holiday Food

Building on gift success: You've learned to create pressure free gift experiences. Now let's tackle another major Christmas challenge: food. Holiday meals combine sensory, social, and routine disruptions that can make eating particularly difficult for autistic children.

Understanding Food Differences During Christmas

For autistic children, food isn't just about hunger or taste. Their brains process sensory information differently, making eating a complex sensory experience. Christmas brings unique food challenges that don't exist during regular family meals: traditional foods appear once a year, meals happen at different times, foods are often mixed together, there's social pressure to try things, regular "safe" foods might not be available, and eating becomes a performance for relatives.

Amy's mom describes it perfectly: "It's not that she's being difficult. For her, the wrong texture feels genuinely painful. The mixed smells of different foods on one plate can be overwhelming. When we add the pressure of everyone watching her try 'just one bite' of Christmas pudding, eating becomes impossible."

The Holiday Food Challenge

Christmas foods challenge each sensory system in new ways. Visual differences include unusual colors, presentations, and garnishes. Taste challenges involve new flavors, stronger seasonings, and unusual combinations. Smell complications arise from mixed aromas, stronger cooking scents, and artificial fragrances. Texture problems come from unfamiliar consistencies, temperatures, and serving methods.

Creating Comfortable Food Experiences

Advanced Preparation The Wilson family starts their "Christmas Food Plan" weeks early. Tom's dad explains: "We put a tiny bit of Christmas food on a separate plate near his regular meals. No pressure to try it, just exposure to seeing and smelling it. Sometimes he asks questions about it, sometimes he ignores it. Both responses are perfectly fine."

The Food Photo Album Emma's family creates a digital album of all foods that will appear at Christmas dinner. "She can look at photos of turkey, stuffing, cranberry sauce throughout December. By Christmas Day, she knows exactly what to expect on the table. Familiar foods feel safer than surprise foods."

Cooking Involvement Max loves helping cook Christmas foods even though he won't eat them. His dad explains: "He can touch, smell, and see them in a controlled way. Sometimes cooking involvement leads to trying, but we never expect it. The goal is familiarity, not consumption."

Setting Up For Success

Safety Stations Lisa created "food safety zones" at family gatherings. "We always make sure there's a quiet place to eat, away from the main table if needed. We bring familiar plates and utensils from home. Most importantly, we always have his preferred foods available. These aren't backup foods or last resorts. They're his Christmas foods, just as valid as anyone else's choices."

The Familiar Food Approach Jake's family learned to "Christmas-ify" his safe foods. "He loves chicken nuggets, so we cut them into star shapes. His usual pasta gets red and green sauce options. It lets him feel part of the celebration while eating foods his body accepts."

Managing Social Pressure

Help relatives understand by being proactive. James's mom sends a gentle note before gatherings: "We explain that pressure makes eating harder, not easier. We ask them to focus on enjoying Maya's company rather than monitoring what she eats. When there's no food pressure, she's actually more likely to try new things on her own timeline."

Family Education Scripts Before gatherings: "Maya experiences food differently than other children. Commenting on her eating makes it harder for her to try new things." During meals: "Let's focus on enjoying each other's company rather than what anyone's eating."

Addressing Specific Holiday Food Challenges

Traditional Christmas Dinner The progressive dinner approach works for many families. Sophie's parents explain: "We do Christmas dinner in courses spread throughout the day. Appetizers at noon, main course at 3, dessert at 6. She can participate in whatever feels manageable without pressure to eat everything at once."

The Tasting Plate Method Instead of expecting Emma to eat a full Christmas dinner, her family creates a "tasting plate" with tiny portions of each dish. "Even touching food with her fork counts as exploration. There's no pressure to actually eat anything."

Holiday Desserts and Treats Max loves decorating cookies but won't eat them. His dad explains: "We use washable food coloring and let him create art. The cookies become decorations rather than food pressure. He gets to participate in the tradition without sensory stress."

Alternative Meal Approaches

Christmas Breakfast Peter's family switched to Christmas breakfast instead of dinner. "It's when he's most relaxed, his safe foods are breakfast foods anyway, and everyone still gets to eat together. We realized it's not about what we eat. It's about being together."

Theme Meals Some families completely reimagine their celebrations. "Our son loves pizza, so we do Christmas pizza night," one family shares. "We use red and green toppings, make it special with nice plates, and everyone enjoys it. Traditional food wasn't bringing joy to our family, so we created our own tradition."

When Things Get Challenging

Watch for signs that your approach needs adjustment: increased anxiety around mealtimes, refusing to eat in social situations, physical signs of stress during meals, complete food refusal, or increased rigidity about food rules.

Quick Response Strategies Have familiar foods readily available, create quiet eating spaces immediately, use familiar plates and utensils, allow flexible eating times, remove all pressure to "perform" at mealtimes, and implement sensory breaks before and after meals.

Supporting Independence

Lauren's teenage son learned to handle food offers politely. "We taught him to say 'No thank you, I'm good with what I have' or 'Maybe later.' It gives him control while being socially appropriate."

For younger children, simple scripts work: "No thank you" or "I'm full." For older children and teens, self-advocacy phrases help them navigate different situations while understanding their own food sensitivities.

Creating New Food Traditions

The goal isn't to force your child to embrace traditional Christmas foods. It's about creating positive food experiences that work for your family. When we focus on connection rather than consumption, meals become opportunities for joy rather than battles.

Food Success Strategies:

- Start food exposure weeks before Christmas
- Always have safe foods available without stigma
- Create quiet, pressure free eating spaces
- Remove social pressure around food choices
- Focus on participation over consumption
- Educate family members about food differences

- Celebrate small steps and exploration
- Consider alternative meal timings and formats

All Together Now Maybe: Managing Family Gatherings

Building on food success: You've learned to remove pressure from eating. Now we'll tackle the most complex Christmas challenge: family gatherings. These events combine every difficulty we've discussed in one high stakes social situation.

Understanding the Social Complexity

Christmas gatherings create unique challenges because they combine multiple social demands with sensory challenges and routine disruptions. Your autistic child must simultaneously process multiple conversations, read complex social cues, manage sensory input, navigate unfamiliar expectations, and handle changes to routine.

Maria describes her 13-year-old son Jake's experience: "It's not that Jake doesn't want to see family. It's that everything happens at once. Aunt Sarah wants a hug, cousins are playing loudly, Grandma's asking questions about school, and someone's wearing strong perfume. It's like asking him to take a math test while riding a rollercoaster."

The Invisible Effort

Family gatherings often represent the most intense situations where autistic children work to appear "normal." This invisible effort, called masking, requires enormous mental energy and often leads to delayed reactions.

Jennifer learned to recognize the signs with her son Marcus: "Marcus would hold it together beautifully at Christmas parties. He'd say thank you for gifts, hug relatives, participate in activities. But I could see the cost. His hands would shake slightly when he thought no one was looking. He'd excuse himself to the bathroom repeatedly, just for quiet moments. By the time we got to the car, he was completely depleted."

Creating a Social Safety Net

Preparing Your Child The Thompson family created their "Party Plan." Before any gathering, they review three key elements. First, they look at photos of who's coming and practice greeting options. High fives are fine if hugs feel overwhelming. Second, they create a signal David can use when he needs a break. Third, they set up his quiet space in advance and practice using it.

Social Rehearsal Emma's family practices gathering scenarios starting two weeks early. "We role-play greeting relatives, answering questions about school, and using polite ways to leave conversations. By the gathering, these interactions feel familiar instead of scary."

Gathering Intelligence Sophie helps research the gathering in advance. Her parents explain: "We find out who's coming, what activities are planned, what food will be served, and how long we'll stay. She becomes a 'gathering detective' rather than someone things are happening to."

Preparing Your Family

Rachel took a proactive approach with relatives. "I wrote an email explaining how Amy experiences social situations differently. I included specific ways they could help, like giving her time to respond to questions and respecting her space preferences. The response was amazing. Family members actually appreciated knowing how to make things easier."

Family Education Templates Instead of lists of restrictions, share what your child loves. "Max enjoys building with cousins, helping in the kitchen, and showing his rock collection. He succeeds when he gets advance notice of activities and regular quiet check-in times."

Helper Roles Give relatives specific supportive jobs. "Uncle Tim becomes the 'quiet activity coordinator,' Aunt Lisa handles the 'snack station,' Grandma hosts the 'story corner.' When everyone has a role supporting Jake, it feels collaborative rather than accommodating."

Making Gatherings Manageable

The Gradual Approach Instead of one overwhelming family explosion, consider spreading celebrations out. Marcus's dad explains: "We now do Christmas in shifts. Grandparents come early for quiet breakfast, aunts and uncles join for lunch, cousins come later for games. Marcus can handle each group better because it's not everyone at once."

The Staging Strategy Tom's family creates natural "acts" in their gathering. "Act 1 is arrival and settling in. Act 2 is structured activities. Act 3 is free play time. Act 4 is meal time. Having clear segments helps Tom know what's expected and when things will change."

Activity Stations Lucy's family sets up different areas: a quiet craft table, a movie corner with headphones, a puzzle zone. "It gives structure to the gathering and means Lucy can participate while managing her social energy. She's not forced to be 'on' constantly."

Time and Energy Management

Consider timing carefully. Sophie's parents learned this through experience: "We discovered Sophie manages better at morning gatherings when she's fresh. We also set clear start and end times. Knowing there's a finish line helps her pace herself."

Energy-Based Scheduling Plan the most challenging parts of gatherings for when your child has the most energy. "Gift opening and group photos happen early when Ben is fresh. By afternoon, we transition to quieter, more individual activities."

Environmental Setup for Success

Sensory-Smart Spaces Use lamps instead of overhead lights to create a calmer atmosphere. Have "quiet conversation" zones and "active play" zones so people who want to chat can do so without competing with loud activities. Limit the number of people in any one room to prevent crowding.

Sound and Light Control The Martinez family discovered that more than six people in a space becomes overwhelming for Miguel, so they encourage natural distribution throughout the house. They also use soft lighting and minimize background noise.

When Things Get Challenging

The Traffic Light System Emma wears a bracelet with different colored beads. She can show green (I'm good), yellow (I need support soon), or red (I need to leave now). Family members watch for her signals and respond immediately without questions.

The 15-Minute Rule Alex's mom checks in subtly every 15 minutes. "A thumbs up means he's good, thumbs down means we activate our escape plan. No questions asked, no pressure to continue."

Unwanted Physical Contact Tom's family developed a simple script: "Tom prefers high fives to hugs right now. It helps him feel more comfortable saying hello." This approach is direct, positive, and easy for relatives to understand.

Managing Extended Family Dynamics

Addressing Resistance When relatives struggle to understand accommodations, focus on outcomes. "We show them how much more Jake participates when his needs are met versus when we try to force traditional approaches."

Building Allies Find family members who naturally understand and ask for their help. "Uncle David became Jake's gathering buddy, understanding his needs and helping other relatives understand too."

Boundary Setting Sometimes firm boundaries are necessary. "If someone won't respect her need for space or continues pressuring her to eat certain foods, we limit their interaction or leave if necessary."

Alternative Gathering Approaches

Small Group Celebrations Instead of one large gathering, do multiple small ones. "Two or three relatives at a time feels manageable, and Ben can actually engage with people instead of just surviving the experience."

Activity-Based Gatherings Organize gatherings around activities Sophie enjoys. "A trip to the science museum with cousins, or a cookie-decorating afternoon. Having a clear purpose and activity helps her navigate the social aspects."

Virtual Participation Some family members join gatherings virtually. "Grandparents who live far away can video call in for gift opening or dinner. It lets Jake connect with them without adding to the in-person social demands."

Building Long-Term Success

The goal isn't perfect family gatherings. It's creating opportunities for authentic connection where your child can be themselves while family members learn to understand and support their needs.

Gathering Success Strategies:

- Prepare both your child and family members in advance

- Create structured activities and designated quiet spaces

- Use timing strategically around your child's energy patterns

- Have clear signals and escape plans ready

- Focus on quality connections over quantity of interactions

- Build in recovery time after social events

- Celebrate participation over performance
- Adapt traditional expectations to fit your family's needs

Remember: The most meaningful family connections often happen in the quiet moments between activities, when children feel safe enough to be themselves.

Surviving the Holiday Hustle: Shopping with Sensory Smarts

Building on social success: You've learned to navigate family gatherings. Now let's tackle shopping, which combines sensory challenges with social pressures in unpredictable public environments.

Understanding the Shopping Challenge

Christmas shopping combines multiple difficulties for autistic children: unpredictable environments, crowd navigation, sensory overload, and changes in routine. It's not just about buying presents. It's about processing overwhelming amounts of information while managing public behavior expectations.

Shopping challenges every sensory system simultaneously. Stores assault children with bright fluorescent lights, flashing signs, crowded aisles, and overwhelming product displays. The auditory environment includes Christmas music, announcement systems, cash registers, crowd noise, and crying children. Different flooring textures, crowded spaces with bumping, product handling, and temperature changes create tactile challenges. Perfumes from cosmetic counters, food court smells, cleaning products, and artificial scents overwhelm the olfactory system.

Real Shopping Experiences

Maria's experience illustrates this perfectly: "Ten minutes into our mall visit, Jake was already overwhelmed. The music was loud, the lights were bright, people kept bumping into him, and the food court smells were mixing together. He went from excited about shopping to complete sensory overload before we even reached our first store."

For children with ADHD, hyperactivity increases in stimulating store environments, impulse control becomes harder around desired items, and staying focused on shopping goals becomes nearly impossible. For children with anxiety, anticipatory worry builds about crowds and unfamiliar environments, fear of getting lost creates constant stress, and social anxiety about interactions with store personnel adds pressure.

Planning Your Shopping Mission

The Reconnaissance Approach The Martinez family revolutionized their shopping experience with "Operation Preview." Carlos's mom explains: "Before our actual shopping trip, we do a 'practice run' during quiet hours. We visit the store when it's less busy, walk our planned route, and take photos of key locations. The entrance we'll use, where we'll park, which aisles we need. Carlos helps create a visual map for our real shopping mission."

Store Research Study store layouts online and call ahead to ask about quieter shopping times. Some stores have sensory-friendly hours or can tell you when they're least crowded. Research exactly where items are located so you can plan efficient routes that minimize time in overwhelming environments.

Timing Strategy Sarah discovered the power of strategic timing: "We learned that Tuesday mornings are quietest at our local mall. We go right when stores open, before the Christmas music starts blasting and crowds build up. Those first peaceful hours make all the difference."

Track crowd patterns at different stores. Grocery stores are calmest early morning, toy stores are quieter mid-week afternoons, and department stores are best right at opening on weekdays.

Making Shopping Manageable

The Mission Control Method The Thompson family created their "Shopping Command Center." Jamie has his tablet with their shopping list app and is in charge of checking items off as they find them. Having this job gives him focus beyond the overwhelming environment. Plus, he wears noise-canceling headphones and has his comfort toy in his backpack. "He's like a special agent on a mission rather than a kid being dragged around shops."

Role Assignment Give everyone specific jobs. "Max is the 'list manager,' Mom is the 'navigator,' Dad is the 'bag carrier.' Having clear roles helps Max feel important and gives structure to the chaos."

Shopping Goals and Rewards Set specific, achievable goals for each shopping trip. "Visit three stores, buy two gifts, stay calm during checkout. When goals are met, there's a predetermined reward like stopping for a favorite snack."

Creating Success Stations

Lisa developed "Recharge Points" throughout the shopping center. "We identify quiet spots: the library corner, calm seating areas, even our car in the parking lot. These become designated break spots. We take five-minute breathers at each one, even if things are going well. Prevention works better than crisis management."

Sensory Break Planning Map sensory breaks into your shopping route. "Every 15-20 minutes, we have a planned stop at a quieter location. Sometimes it's sitting on a bench, sometimes it's stepping outside, sometimes it's visiting the bookstore which is naturally calmer."

Portable Calm Kits Tom carries a small backpack with his sensory tools: noise-canceling headphones, fidget toys, water bottle, and snack. "Having his tools accessible helps him self-regulate throughout the shopping trip."

Alternative Shopping Strategies

The Online Option Involving Max in online shopping teaches valuable skills. His dad shares: "He learns about budgeting, making choices, and waiting for delivery. Plus, he can take his time deciding without pressure. We make it special: hot chocolate, comfy sofa, and his favorite music playing softly while we shop together on the tablet."

Hybrid Approaches Combine online research with targeted store visits. "Sophie researches products online, reads reviews, and narrows down choices. Then we make quick, focused store visits to see final options in person before ordering online."

The Divide and Conquer Method Emma's parents found a practical solution: "One parent takes Emma to do her carefully planned shopping trip, while the other handles the more chaotic shopping elements. Emma gets to participate in Christmas preparations without becoming overwhelmed, and we get everything done."

Managing Challenging Situations

When Things Get Overwhelming Keep an "Exit Kit" ready: favorite calming toy, water bottle, small snack, emergency headphones, and car keys easily accessible. If you spot early warning signs, you can quickly activate your escape plan.

The 5-4-3-2-1 Grounding Technique When Sophie starts getting overwhelmed, her parents use sensory grounding: "Find 5 things you can see, 4 things you can touch, 3 things you can hear, 2 things you can smell, 1 thing you can taste. It helps her reconnect with her body and calm down."

Store Staff Communication Learn to quickly explain your situation to store employees. "Most are very understanding when we say 'My son has autism and is getting overwhelmed. Can you help us find a quiet spot?' People want to help when they understand."

Building Shopping Skills Over Time

Skill Progression Start with five-minute store visits just to walk through and leave. Then ten-minute visits to buy one predetermined item. Then 15-minute visits for two items. Build your child's shopping tolerance gradually.

Independence Development As Sophie got older, her parents taught her to advocate for her own needs while shopping. "She can ask store employees for help, use store restrooms when needed, and communicate when she needs a break."

Budget Management Ben learns about money management through Christmas shopping. His parents explain: "He has a specific budget for each family member and practices making choices within those limits. Shopping becomes a real-world math and life skills lesson."

Creating Positive Shopping Memories

Success Celebrations After successful shopping trips, celebrate specific achievements: staying calm during checkout, trying on new clothes, or helping choose a gift for someone else. "Recognizing these successes builds confidence for future shopping."

Building Shopping Traditions Create positive shopping traditions: annual trips for specific items, special shopping snacks, or visiting favorite stores. "These traditions help Sophie associate shopping with positive experiences rather than stress."

Gift Solutions Beyond Shopping

Creative Alternatives Jake makes photo books for family members instead of buying traditional gifts. "He selects photos, arranges layouts, and creates personalized gifts that use his strengths while avoiding overwhelming shopping experiences."

Experience Gifts Focus on giving experiences rather than things: tickets to museums, zoo memberships, or activity vouchers. "These can often be purchased online and avoid both shopping stress and gift-wrapping challenges."

Service Projects Ben chooses charity organizations to support instead of buying gifts for extended family. "He researches causes he cares about and makes donations in family members' names. It connects to his values while avoiding shopping stress."

Shopping Success Strategies:

- Start with reconnaissance visits during quiet times

- Plan routes and identify sensory break spots
- Use technology tools for preparation and support
- Have clear exit strategies and communication plans
- Build shopping tolerance gradually over time
- Focus on participation over purchasing perfection
- Celebrate small successes and learning moments
- Adapt traditional shopping approaches to fit your child's needs

The goal is helping your child develop skills and confidence to participate in community activities while honoring their sensory and emotional needs.

ROOM FOR ALL THE REINDEER: INCLUDING SIBLINGS IN THE SEASON

Building on community success: You've learned to navigate public spaces. Now let's address how Christmas accommodations affect siblings and how to create celebrations where every family member feels valued.

The Complex Reality of Sibling Dynamics

Siblings of autistic children navigate Christmas with their own unique challenges and gifts. While much attention focuses on supporting the autistic child through the holidays, siblings experience their own complex emotional journey that deserves understanding and support.

Every accommodation impacts siblings. When celebrations are modified for sensory needs, siblings experience different family traditions than their friends. When social events are adjusted for comfort levels, siblings sometimes miss activities they'd enjoy. When meltdowns occur during family time, siblings witness stress and may feel responsible for maintaining peace.

Understanding the Sibling Experience

Jenny, mother to Tom (autistic, 9) and Sarah (11), shares: "Sarah once told me she feels like Christmas comes with an invisible rulebook. All the things we can't do, or have to do differently. She loves her brother but sometimes wishes we could just have a 'regular' Christmas like her friends."

Siblings often experience pride and protectiveness toward their autistic sibling, frustration when celebrations are modified, guilt about wanting traditional Christmas experiences, extra responsibility for their sibling's wellbeing, confusion about family rules and expectations, maturity beyond their years in understanding differences, and deep empathy and advocacy skills.

Developmental Considerations

Young Siblings (Ages 3-7) May not fully understand why accommodations are needed, might feel jealous of special attention given to autistic sibling, need simple explanations about differences, benefit from their own special roles and responsibilities, and require extra reassurance about family love and stability.

School-Age Siblings (Ages 8-12) Begin understanding autism more deeply, may feel embarrassed by public meltdowns or different family approaches, develop strong protective instincts, need opportunities for conventional experiences with peers, and benefit from education about autism and advocacy skills.

Teen Siblings (Ages 13+) Face social pressures about family differences, may take on caregiver roles inappropriately, need support in developing their own identity separate from family dynamics, benefit from connection with other sibling support groups, and require guidance in setting healthy boundaries.

The Hidden Emotional Work

Siblings often take on invisible emotional labor during Christmas:

Social Translation Emma automatically explains to her friends why their Christmas is different. "She's become our family's interpreter, helping others understand why we do things differently."

Emotional Support "When I see Ben getting overwhelmed, I know to go get his headphones or suggest we move to a quieter room," his 10-year-old sister shares. "I can tell before Mom and Dad sometimes."

Advocacy and Protection "If someone at school says something mean about our family's Christmas traditions, Sophie defends us," her parents note. "She's become a fierce advocate for autism acceptance."

Creating Balance Through Understanding

Open Communication The Williams family introduced "Christmas Chats." Every Sunday in December, they have special one-on-one time with each child. "It's a chance for both kids to share their feelings about the season without worry. Lucy can express excitement about parties without feeling guilty, and we can help Jake process his concerns about changes."

Family Meetings "We hold weekly family meetings where everyone gets equal time to share," the Thompson family explains. "Each person gets five minutes to talk about their week, their feelings, and their needs. It ensures both children feel heard and valued."

Emotion Validation "We teach all our children that feelings are valid, even when they're conflicting," Maria shares. "Sophie can love her brother AND feel frustrated about missing a party. Both feelings are okay and normal."

Sibling-Only Time Schedule regular time for just your non-autistic children. "Time to express feelings they might not share in front of their autistic sibling, and time to just be kids without thinking about accommodations."

Individual Traditions

Mark and Emma's parents found a beautiful solution with "Special Santa Time." Each child gets their own Christmas moment. Emma has quiet morning gift opening with calming music and no pressure. Later, Mark gets his excited present-ripping session with all the chaos he loves. "They both get their perfect Christmas, just differently."

Personal Christmas Stories "Each child gets to create their own Christmas narrative," the Wilson family shares. "Sophie's story includes quiet magic and gentle surprises. Max's story includes exciting adventures and loud celebrations. Both stories are equally important in our family."

Special Roles "Tom becomes 'Christmas Morning Photographer' while his sister gets to be 'Present Distribution Manager,'" their parents explain. "Each child has a special role that makes them feel important and needed."

The Team Approach

The Anderson family developed "Christmas Crews." Instead of dividing the family, they paired the kids up as holiday helpers. Josh helps Amy manage noisy gatherings by being her "quiet zone buddy," while Amy helps Josh organize his gift list because she's great with details. "They've learned to use each other's strengths."

Complementary Skills "Emma's organization skills help Ben prepare for Christmas events, while Ben's detailed knowledge helps Emma learn interesting facts to share with relatives," their parents explain. "They support each other's strengths instead of focusing on challenges."

Understanding Fair vs Equal

"We had to learn that fair doesn't mean identical," shares David's dad. "Some days, Michael needs more attention to handle Christmas events. Other days, Lisa needs extra time to process her feelings about changed plans. Fair means giving each child what they need, when they need it."

Resource Allocation "We explain to our children that fairness means everyone gets what they need to be successful," the Martinez family shares. "Sometimes that means Ben gets noise-canceling headphones for the Christmas concert while his sister gets to invite friends. Different tools, same goal of everyone enjoying themselves."

Supporting Siblings' Individual Needs

Education and Understanding Help siblings understand autism in age-appropriate ways. "We explain to Emma that Ben's brain processes Christmas differently," their mom explains. "It's like Ben has super-sensitive Christmas sensors. He notices lights, sounds, and changes more than most people. Understanding this helps Emma be more patient and proud of how Ben manages challenges."

For Young Children Use simple explanations. "Max's brain is like a computer that processes information differently. Sometimes it needs extra time or different input to work best."

For School-Age Children "Sophie learns about sensory processing, executive function, and social communication," her parents share. "Understanding the science helps her feel proud of her knowledge and confident in explaining autism to friends."

For Teenagers "Emma reads books by autistic authors and follows autism advocates on social media," her mom explains. "She's developing her own understanding of autism beyond just her brother's experience."

Individual Space and Time

Create opportunities for non-autistic siblings to have their own Christmas experiences. "Sophie gets to choose one 'full Christmas' event each year," her mom shares. "She might pick a school carol concert or a busy Santa visit. Something we know would be too much for Jack. She goes with grandparents or just one parent, so she can fully enjoy it without worrying about her brother."

Peer Activities "Tom gets to have friends over for traditional Christmas activities that would be too overwhelming for his autistic sister," his parents explain. "Cookie decorating parties, loud Christmas movies, chaotic gift exchanges. He gets to experience 'typical' Christmas fun with peers."

Extended Family Connections "Sophie spends Christmas Eve with her grandparents doing traditional activities," her family shares. "It gives her the conventional Christmas experience she craves while allowing us to create a calm Christmas morning for her brother."

Managing Difficult Emotions

When Resentment Rises Karen developed a system for her children called "feeling baubles." Red for angry, blue for sad, gold for happy. "The kids can hang them on a small tree in their rooms when they need to express emotions without words. It helps us know when they need extra support or attention."

Emotional Validation Processes "We have a family rule that all feelings are welcome and valid," the Thompson family explains. "Lisa can say 'I'm mad that we can't go to the loud Christmas party' and we respond with 'That makes sense. It's okay to feel disappointed' before problem-solving together."

Emotional Release Activities "When Sophie feels frustrated about accommodations, she has healthy ways to express it," her parents share. "She might write in her journal, create art about her feelings, or have a good cry with Mom. Rather than 'correcting' her emotions, we offer comfort and space to feel them fully.

Celebrating Different Successes

"We made our own advent calendar," explains Peter's mom. "Each day has two pockets, one for each child. The treats inside are different because the kids have different interests, but they're equally special. It teaches them that different can still be wonderful."

Achievement Recognition "We celebrate Ben's success in staying calm during a family gathering with equal enthusiasm as we celebrate his sister's success in her school Christmas performance," their parents explain. "Different achievements, same pride and recognition."

Building Sibling Bonds

Joint Projects "The kids work together on a family Christmas video each year," Tom's family shares. "His sister directs and edits while Tom contributes his knowledge about technical details. It's become a treasured family tradition that uses both their strengths."

Sibling Gift Exchanges "Emma and Ben have their own private gift exchange," their parents explain. "They choose gifts specifically for each other based on their real interests and needs. It strengthens their bond and shows how well they understand each other."

Shared Traditions "Both children contribute to our family Christmas story book," the Wilson family shares. "They take turns writing chapters about our Christmas adventures, creating a shared narrative that honors both their perspectives."

Warning Signs

Watch for increased sibling conflict during Christmas season, withdrawal from family activities by non-autistic siblings, expression of unfairness or resentment, changes in behavior or mood in either child, reluctance to participate in modified celebrations, regression in sibling relationship quality, excessive caretaking behaviors by non-autistic siblings, academic or social problems at school, or sleep and appetite changes during holiday season.

Support Considerations "We got Sophie counseling when we noticed she was taking on too much responsibility for her brother's emotional regulation," her parents share. "She needed help learning healthy boundaries and developing her own identity."

"Connecting Emma with other siblings of autistic children was life-changing," her mom explains. "She realized she wasn't alone in her experiences and learned coping strategies from other kids who understood."

Creating Long-Term Success

Teaching Acceptance "We focus on teaching our children that different doesn't mean less than," Maria explains. "Sophie understands that her brother's way of experiencing Christmas isn't wrong, just different. This acceptance will serve their relationship for life."

Developing Independence "We make sure Tom develops his own interests and friendships separate from his role as his brother's sibling," his parents share. "While we want them to support each other, we don't want his identity to be solely defined by having an autistic brother."

Moving Forward as a Family Remember, successful family celebrations don't mean everyone does everything together all the time. Success means creating space for each child to experience and enjoy Christmas in their own way while maintaining family connections.

The Thompson family's motto sums it up beautifully: "In our family, Christmas is like a puzzle. Each person's piece looks different, but they all fit together to make something beautiful."

Sibling Support Strategies:

- Validate all emotions as normal and acceptable
- Create individual traditions alongside family ones
- Provide education about autism appropriate to each child's age
- Ensure one on one time with each child

- Celebrate different types of successes equally
- Build advocacy skills and confidence
- Connect siblings with peers who have similar experiences
- Maintain realistic expectations for sibling relationships

TECH THE HALLS: USING TECHNOLOGY TO SUPPORT SUCCESS

Building on family harmony: You've learned to support all your children's needs. Now let's explore how technology can enhance your Christmas strategies without replacing human connection.

Understanding Technology's Role

Technology isn't just about screen time during Christmas. It's about creating predictability, providing communication tools, and offering safe spaces to practice holiday scenarios. Used thoughtfully, technology becomes a powerful tool for navigating Christmas challenges.

Technology can support every strategy we've discussed. Visual schedules and countdown timers help with transitions. Apps for calming, noise cancellation, and environmental control support sensory management. Social stories and expectation setting help with gift preparation. Menu previews and restaurant research support food planning. Photo books and conversation practice help with social preparation.

For children with ADHD, timers and alerts help with attention and transitions, interactive apps provide appropriate stimulation, and visual reminders support executive function challenges. For children with anxiety, predictable information reduces worry about unknowns, practice apps allow rehearsing scenarios safely, and having control over information reduces anticipatory stress.

Digital Tools for Christmas Success

Visual Schedules and Countdowns The Martinez family created their "Christmas Command Center" app. Miguel's mom shares: "We use a digital calendar that Miguel can check anytime. It shows exactly what's happening each day with pictures and videos from previous years. The predictability helps him feel secure even when routines change."

Sync your Christmas schedule across all devices. "His tablet, our phones, even the kitchen display shows the same information. Wherever he is, he can check what's coming next."

Sophie loves countdown apps. Her dad shares: "She has different countdowns for different events. Three days until Grandma visits, six hours until gift opening, 30 minutes until dinner. It helps her prepare mentally for transitions."

Each calendar entry can link to photos, videos, or documents about that activity. "If we're going to cousin Sarah's house, he can click and see photos of her house, her family, and what activities we'll do there."

Social Story Apps and Preparation Tools Lisa discovered the power of digital social stories. "We created personalized stories about our family Christmas using photos and videos. Emma can review them whenever she feels anxious about upcoming events. It's like having a rehearsal guide for the holidays."

Take photos throughout December to create stories for next year. "Pictures of him successfully opening gifts, enjoying family dinner, playing with cousins. Seeing himself succeed helps him feel confident about doing it again."

Max loves watching videos of previous Christmas celebrations. "We edit them to show positive moments and successful strategies. It's like having a highlight reel of Christmas success."

Use apps that let children choose different paths through social situations. "If Aunt Mary wants to hug you, you can choose: high five, hug, or wave. It helps him practice making social choices."

Communication and Support Apps Emma has communication cards on her tablet for Christmas situations. "I need a break, This is too loud, Thank you, I like this. She can show adults what she needs without having to find words when stressed."

Create family apps where anyone can send quick alerts. "Code yellow means someone needs support soon, code red means we need to leave immediately. Everyone gets the message instantly."

The kids use messaging apps to support each other during stressful events. "They can send encouraging messages or request help without disrupting family activities."

Sensory Support Apps Jake wears bluetooth headphones connected to his tablet. "He can switch between noise canceling mode, calming music, or white noise depending on what the environment needs."

Load tablets with breathing apps, meditation games, and favorite calming videos. "When she starts feeling overwhelmed, she knows exactly where to find her calming tools."

Use apps that monitor sound levels in your house. "When noise gets too high, the app alerts us to turn down music or move to quieter spaces before Tom gets overwhelmed."

Planning and Organization Apps "Our whole family uses the same Christmas planning app," the Wilson family explains. "It tracks gift lists, menu planning, guest lists, and schedules. Max can check who's coming to dinner and what food will be served."

Emma loves the gift budget app. "She can track spending for each family member and make sure gifts are fair and within budget. It appeals to her sense of order and justice."

Use store apps that show exactly where items are located. "Jake can see the store map, locate the items we need, and plan our route. It makes shopping feel like a mission instead of chaos."

Educational and Practice Apps

Holiday Learning Games Max uses apps to learn about different Christmas traditions around the world. "It connects to his love of geography and helps him understand why families do things differently."

Sophie loves following recipe apps to help with Christmas baking. "The step-by-step photos and timers help her contribute to holiday preparations in a way that works for her brain."

Find apps that let children practice conversations and social scenarios. "Ben can rehearse greeting relatives, asking for help, and expressing gratitude in a low-pressure digital environment."

Managing Screen Time During Holidays

Balanced Technology Use Build in specific technology time rather than having devices compete with family time. "Ben gets 30 minutes with his calming apps after family dinner, then he's ready to engage with people again."

Designate certain areas and times as device-free, but also make sure to have tech-supported calm spaces available when needed.

"Everyone in the family has the same technology guidelines during Christmas," Tom's parents explain. "This helps our autistic son not feel singled out while maintaining healthy boundaries."

Accessibility and Accommodation Tools

Assistive Technology Maya uses her communication device to participate in Christmas conversations. "She can share her excitement about gifts, ask questions about activities, and express her needs clearly."

Use visual timer apps for all transitions. "Getting dressed for church, time until dessert, how long until we leave the party. Visual time helps him manage waiting."

Emma's apps are all customized to her sensory preferences. "Low contrast colors, minimal animation, clear fonts. Her device is set up to support her processing rather than stress it."

Technology Troubleshooting

When Technology Causes Problems Learn the balance between helpful technology and dependence. "Now we gradually introduce situations where he practices managing without his device, but always with it available as backup."

When Ben's device malfunctions during a stressful time, it can trigger a meltdown. "We keep backup devices charged and loaded with the same apps. Technology needs backup plans too."

Some relatives initially objected to technology use during family time. "But when they saw how much it helped Jake participate and enjoy gatherings, they became supportive."

Creating Family Technology Plans

"We created a family contract about technology use during Christmas," the Martinez family explains. "Everyone agrees on when devices are helpful, when they're not appropriate, and how to ask for tech support when needed."

Have clear plans for technology failures. "Backup devices, alternative calming strategies, and ways to continue activities even when technology isn't working."

Looking Ahead

"Each year we update our Christmas apps and stories with new photos and experiences," the Martinez family explains. "It becomes a fun way to reflect on how our son has grown and what strategies now work best."

"We're building a digital Christmas memory book that our children can use with their own families someday," Sophie's parents share. "It includes all the strategies that worked, photos of successful celebrations, and lessons learned."

"As Emma gets older, we're teaching her to choose and manage her own assistive technology," her parents explain. "She's learning to identify what apps help her in different situations and how to advocate for technology accommodations."

Remember that technology should enhance, not replace, human

connection during Christmas. The goal is to use digital tools to reduce stress and increase your child's ability to participate in meaningful holiday experiences.

Technology Success Strategies:

- Use apps to increase predictability and control
- Create digital social stories with family photos
- Have backup devices and plans ready
- Balance screen time with family time
- Customize interfaces to your child's sensory needs
- Use technology to support communication and self advocacy
- Include your child in choosing helpful apps and tools
- Regularly review and update technology strategies
- Teach family members how technology supports your child
- Plan for technology failures with alternative strategies

When thoughtfully integrated, technology becomes not just a tool, but a bridge to greater Christmas enjoyment and family connection.

Creating Your Own Kind of Merry: Autism-Friendly Holiday Traditions

Building on technological support: You've learned to use technology as a tool for success. Now let's explore how to create family traditions that celebrate your unique strengths rather than forcing conformity to conventional expectations.

Reimagining What Traditions Can Be

Traditional Christmas activities often present multiple challenges for autistic children. Waiting to open presents on Christmas morning creates anticipation anxiety and performance pressure. Sitting through long family meals combines food challenges with social demands. Visiting Santa in noisy shopping centers creates sensory overwhelm. Attending crowded carol services brings both social and sensory difficulties.

Maria, mother to Alex (11), shares: "I used to feel guilty about not doing things 'properly.' Then I realized, whose definition of proper? Why are we trying to force traditions that make everyone miserable just because that's how it's always been done?"

Building From Strengths

The Johnson Family Revolution Tom's dad explains their breakthrough: "We stopped trying to modify traditional celebrations and started creating our own. We call it our 'Christmas Your Way' approach. Instead of midnight mass, we have 'Dawn Devotions,' a quiet, peaceful celebration when the church is empty. Tom loves watching the sunrise through the stained glass windows, and it's become our special thing."

Strength-Based Tradition Building "We built traditions around what Alex loves, not what he struggles with," his mom explains. "He loves organizing, so our tradition became creating detailed Christmas plans together. He loves routine, so we do the exact same magical sequence every Christmas morning. His strengths became our family's special traditions."

Sensory-Smart Celebration Design "All our traditions pass the sensory test," Emma's family shares. "If it involves overwhelming lights, sounds, smells, or social pressure, we adapt it until it feels good for everyone. Our Christmas tree has only steady lights, our carols are instrumental, and our gatherings have quiet corners."

Making Magic Manageable

Reimagining Santa The Peterson family reinvented Santa visits with "Santa's Special Delivery." Sarah's mom explains: "Instead of the mall Santa experience, Santa leaves small gifts and clues throughout December, leading to the main presents. Sarah can process each interaction in her own time, without the pressure of a face-to-face meeting, and the anticipation becomes exciting rather than overwhelming."

The Video Message Santa Ben gets personalized video messages from Santa throughout December. "He can watch them as many times as he wants, pause when he needs to process, and there's no social pressure to respond appropriately in the moment."

The Santa Photo Shoot "Instead of a mall Santa visit, we hire a photographer to come to our house," Sophie's family explains. "Santa visits in our sensory-friendly environment, and Sophie can interact or observe from a distance. We get beautiful photos without the overwhelming mall experience."

Creating New Traditions That Work

The Comfort Calendar Lisa developed their "Joy Journey." Each day in December has one small, manageable festive activity. "Some days it's as simple as wearing Christmas socks or having hot chocolate with marshmallows. Other days we might do something more Christmas-themed, but always within Michael's comfort zone. It makes the whole season feel special without being overwhelming."

The Choice Calendar "Each day, Jake chooses from three pre-planned activity options," his mom explains. "A sensory activity, a social activity, and a solo activity. He controls his December experience while still having festive structure."

The Interest-Based Calendar "Every December activity connects to Max's special interests," his dad shares. "Train-themed ornament making, mathematical gift wrapping patterns, scientific investigation of snow. Christmas becomes an extension of what he loves."

Sensory-Friendly Celebrations

The Wilson family created "Silent Night Specials." Every evening, they spend 15 minutes looking at Christmas lights in their pajamas. "No carols, no pressure, just quiet appreciation of the pretty lights. It's become everyone's favorite part of Christmas."

Texture-Free Decorating "Tom helps decorate by directing rather than touching," his family explains. "He tells us where ornaments should go, chooses color schemes, and designs arrangements. He participates fully without sensory stress."

Scent-Free Holiday Baking "We bake with ingredients that don't have strong smells," Emma's family discovered. "Sugar cookies instead of spice cookies, vanilla instead of cinnamon. She can participate in baking without olfactory overwhelm."

Adapting Popular Traditions

The Christmas Eve Box Reimagined "Instead of new pajamas and activities that might feel overwhelming, Emma's box contains her favorite comfort items dressed up for Christmas," her mom explains. "Her regular soft blanket with a festive ribbon, her usual snacks in Christmas containers, her familiar books with holiday bookmarks."

The Advent Calendar Alternative "Instead of chocolate or toys, our advent calendar has activities Sophie chooses," her parents share. "Read a chapter of a favorite book, watch 10 minutes of a preferred video, have a special snack. Each day brings comfort rather than surprise."

Elf on the Shelf Alternatives "Our 'Christmas Mouse' leaves tiny notes and small changes that Ben notices and enjoys," his parents explain. "A new book appears, his favorite snacks are arranged in patterns, or his toys are organized in interesting ways. Magic without pressure."

Carol Services at Home David's family found a beautiful solution: "We have our own carol service at home. David chooses the music, controls the volume, and can stim or move as much as he needs. Sometimes he conducts, sometimes he just listens, but it's always comfortable."

Building Traditions Around Communication Styles

For Non-Speaking Children "Maya's Christmas traditions involve her communication device," her family explains. "She programs holiday messages, chooses music, and shares her excitement through technology. Her voice is central to our celebrations."

For Children with Scripted Speech "We build Ben's favorite phrases and scripts into our traditions," his parents share. "If he always says 'Red truck!' when excited, red trucks become part of our decorating theme. His natural communication becomes our family's special language."

When Extended Family Struggles with Changes

Communication Strategies The Anderson family developed a proactive approach. "We send a 'Christmas Update' email explaining our plans positively: 'This year we're excited to be creating new traditions that work for everyone in our family. We'd love to share them with you, and hear about your special plans too.'"

Including Others in New Traditions "We invite relatives to join our new traditions," shares Mark's dad. "When they see how much more Mark enjoys our quiet Christmas morning walk compared to the chaos of traditional present opening, they understand why we've made changes."

Building Tradition Acceptance "We document our successful traditions with photos and videos," Tom's family explains. "When relatives see how happy and engaged Tom is during our adapted celebrations, they become supporters rather than skeptics."

Technology-Enhanced Traditions

Digital Tradition Documentation "We create annual Christmas videos that become family treasures," Emma's family explains. "Each year adds to our digital collection of successful strategies and happy memories."

Virtual Tradition Sharing "We share our traditions with other autism families through video calls," the Wilson family discovered. "Our children get to see that other families also do Christmas differently, and they feel proud of their unique celebrations."

Evaluating Tradition Success

Look for reduced anxiety about holiday events, increased participation in activities, more genuine enjoyment, fewer meltdowns, family members feeling more relaxed, positive anticipation of celebrations, children asking about or planning for traditions, siblings enjoying adapted celebrations, and extended family understanding and supporting changes.

When Traditions Need Adjustment "Every January, we evaluate what worked and what didn't," Maria shares. "We ask each family member for input and make adjustments for the following year. Traditions should evolve as our children grow."

"Our core traditions stay the same, but we adapt details as needed," David's parents explain. "The structure of our Christmas morning routine remains constant, but we might change the specific activities based on David's current interests and needs."

Building Long-Term Family Identity

Creating Your Family's Christmas Story "We help our children understand that our traditions are special precisely because they work for our family," Tom's parents share. "We're not trying to be like other families. We're celebrating being exactly who we are."

Teaching Tradition Values "Our children learn that traditions should serve people, not the other way around," Sophie's family explains. "If a tradition causes stress or excludes someone, it's not serving our family well and needs to change."

Moving Forward with Your Family's Traditions

Remember, successful traditions don't have to look Instagram-perfect. They just need to work for your family. As Rachel's mom beautifully puts it: "Our Christmas probably looks weird to outsiders. We eat pizza instead of turkey, open presents over several days, and our Christmas tree is blue because that's Rachel's favorite color. But it's perfect for us because everyone can truly enjoy it."

Tradition Building Strategies:

- Start with what your child enjoys and excels at
- Keep sensory needs at the forefront of planning
- Make activities manageable and predictable
- Include elements that provide comfort and security
- Allow for flexibility and individual participation styles
- Create escape routes and backup plans

- Celebrate small victories and genuine moments
- Include all family members in tradition creation
- Document successful approaches for future years
- Be willing to adapt as children grow and change

The Martinez family's motto sums it up perfectly: "Tradition means doing things with love. It doesn't specify exactly what those things need to be."

Remember: The most meaningful traditions are often born from understanding and accepting your family's unique needs rather than forcing conformity to traditional expectations.

When we create traditions that truly work for our families, we're not just making Christmas better. We're teaching our children that they deserve accommodations, that their needs matter, and that families can create joy in many different ways.

Your Family's Perfect Christmas

As we reach the end of this guide, I want you to take a moment to appreciate how far you've come. If you picked up this book feeling overwhelmed by the prospect of Christmas with your autistic child, you now have a comprehensive toolkit of strategies, insights, and hope.

What You've Learned

Through these thirteen chapters, you've gained understanding of:

- The hidden challenges your child faces during Christmas, including the exhausting work of appearing "normal"

- The neurological reality of meltdowns and how they differ from tantrums

- How co-occurring conditions like ADHD and anxiety complicate the holiday season

- Transition strategies that build bridges between routine and celebration

- Sensory accommodations that make festivities accessible

rather than overwhelming

- Gift-giving approaches that reduce pressure while maintaining joy

- Food strategies that honor your child's needs while building family connection

- Social navigation tools for family gatherings that work for everyone

- Shopping techniques that transform stress into success

- Sibling support that ensures every family member feels valued

- Technology integration that enhances rather than replaces human connection

- Tradition creation that celebrates your family's unique strengths and needs

The Ripple Effects

But this knowledge extends far beyond Christmas. The strategies you've learned here will serve your family throughout the year. Understanding meltdowns helps with school transitions, birthday parties, and everyday stress. Sensory accommodations improve daily life, not just holidays. Social preparation techniques support school events, family visits, and community activities.

What Success Really Looks Like

Success isn't about creating a Christmas that looks like anyone else's. Success is:

- Seeing your child genuinely relaxed during family celebrations
- Watching siblings support each other rather than compete for attention
- Feeling confident in your ability to adapt plans when needed
- Experiencing moments of pure joy without the shadow of anxiety
- Building family traditions that everyone can participate in authentically
- Creating memories that feel joyful rather than stressful
- Knowing that your child's needs are understood and respected
- Watching extended family learn to support your child's success

The Deeper Impact

Perhaps most importantly, you've learned that accommodating your child's needs doesn't diminish Christmas magic. It creates a different kind of magic, one that's more inclusive, more authentic, and more sustainable for your family.

You've discovered that when you stop trying to force your child into traditional molds and instead shape celebrations around their strengths, everyone benefits. Siblings learn empathy and creativity. Extended family members develop deeper understanding. Your autistic child experiences belonging rather than just survival.

Moving Forward

As you implement these strategies, remember that progress isn't always linear. Some Christmases will go more smoothly than others. Some strategies will work perfectly one year and need adjustment the next. This isn't failure. It's the natural process of growing and adapting with your child.

Keep what works, adapt what doesn't, and don't be afraid to try new approaches. Your child is constantly developing, and your family's needs will evolve. The goal isn't to find the perfect system and stick with it forever. The goal is to maintain the flexibility and understanding that allows you to create joy for your family, however that looks.

Your Family's Legacy

The accommodations you make for Christmas today are teaching your child invaluable lessons about advocacy, acceptance, and the importance of honoring everyone's needs. You're showing them that families can be creative, that different doesn't mean less than, and that love means making space for each person to be themselves.

You're also modeling for siblings how to support family members with different needs, how to find creative solutions to challenges, and how to celebrate uniqueness rather than conformity.

A Final Thought

If there's one thing I hope you take from this book, it's this: there is no "right" way to do Christmas. There's only your family's way. And when your family's way honors each person's needs, celebrates everyone's strengths, and creates space for authentic joy, that's not just a successful Christmas. That's a beautiful way to live.

Your child doesn't need to change to deserve a magical Christmas. Christmas needs to change to include your magical child.

Here's to your family's perfectly imperfect, wonderfully unique, absolutely right-for-you Christmas. May it be filled with understanding, acceptance, and moments of pure joy, however they might look.

www.ingramcontent.com/pod-product-compliance
Lightning Source LLC
Chambersburg PA
CBHW020545080526
44583CB00013B/1006